ISBN: 979-8-218-86158-2
First Edition

For permissions, inquiries, or licensing:
dustywilsonproductions@outlook.com

Printed in the United States of America.

"Everything in this book is up for interpretation."

Siegfried
AN INTRODUCTION

Look at the stars —
weeping in the sky.
A burning heart,
or an aching lie.

Loving you —
I can't let go.
Yet I never did know
why you wouldn't show.

Your linen and curls,
your soft white pearls —
yet I never did know…

Did you know me?
Siegfried.

— Dusty Wilson

Everything in this book is up for interpretation.

This is a work of creative expression. Names, characters, places, and incidents are either used fictitiously or are a product of the author's experience and interpretation. Any resemblance to actual persons, living or dead, is coincidental.

Trigger Warning:
Contains themes of mental health, identity conflict, spirituality, and emotional trauma.

Siegfried

Written and Produced by Dusty Wilson

11/08/2025

The expectations of who the world wishes I were in comparison to the truth of my life.

Siegfried is a Germanic and Nordic mythological character that represents pure masculinity and strength. A mold that I was not made to fit- nor could I ever even try.

Sections

-Identity

-Outside

-Philosophy

-Love

-Family

-Society

-Warfare

IDENTITY

The identity of Dusty Wilson

SECTION I

"Everything that a man should be"

Identity

Everything that a man should be —
there you were,
standing with me.

Knowing,
yet keeping it to myself.
Why must our words hold weight
if only they are just letters on paper?

Who decides what that makes them?
They take away our worth
and can give it back too —
with the weight of a hammer,
but light as a feather.

Just like a man
and his social endeavors.
You might sit there and wonder —
just look for a while.

A man cannot mourn.
There is no reconcile —
no time to fit in,
or even be cut out.

Like words on a page
you say,
"You'll never be enough for me."

And I cried,
but only when I could be free.

—Dusty Wilson

Insomnia
Identity

I toss and I turn —
I beg to fall asleep.
I can't turn away,
can't try to hear you weep.

You know it breaks my heart —
it would be so,
if I could find myself
without letting you know.

Lead me on —
give me candy and a show.
I'll sit down and cry,
and we could join as brothers.

A devil's advocate
cannot be from my mother —
though we are another.
Cannot be departed,
for I would mourn
and beg to be broken-hearted.

Away in my slumber —
a blonde beauty lay.
With light in that rearview
on a soft summer's day.

You reap what you sow,
and you can't turn away.

— Dusty Wilson

Timeless
Identity

It's all about love, until you're unfamiliar —
a type that doesn't,
it doesn't fit your mold.

So I sit and I shout
while you scream from without,
and within your mind leans.

You say that you
never are *for,*
but can't find it within —
your life is a bore.

Your soul is a grave,
a tomb, unsaved.

So you sit and you mock —
you mock and you gawk.

The pity and prejudice,
on most high is your pride —
and your tail you cannot hide.

So come out, all
you who are within.
Let's make them fall,
so they realize their sin.

Without you — who are,
and who are from within,
a child cries out —
he can never win.

— Dusty Wilson

Mirror
Identity

When I look in my reflection,
I cannot see
the version of me
that I call my own.

There were highs,
and there were lows —
all that I know
is I can't let it go.

I kiss my reflection,
but it won't kiss back.
My warm, soft lips
touch the cold, hard glass.

And it leaves an imprint —
a stain for a second.
And then I'm reminded:
my mirror can't breathe.

Why, oh why, am I always caught in daydreams?
With candlelit dinners
and carnival rides —
or even just the simpler nights.

I'll hold myself forever —
I can't let go.
It's all I've ever known,
and I hate myself so.

— Dusty Wilson

Being Me
Identity

I notice the way that people look at me
differently —
that smirk,
that smile,
that hatred heart.

They say they can *smell the Spirit,*
or I have a certain look,
when I'm just me —
and I can't escape my skin.

I don't know why I stay,
and I don't know how to change.
I just wish I was normal.

These people hurt me,
ostracize my heart
until it's black and blue —
and I fall apart.

— Dusty Wilson

Everything I Do
Identity

Why is everything I do
so evil to you?

I thought that you'd be somebody —
someone to understand,
but you put me in this body,
put me in my place.

I feel like I was
just a disgrace.

Why can't anybody
even look me in the face?

—Dusty Wilson

At Least You Grew Into Your Shoes
Identity

My soul is in the back,
my heart is in the front of my mind —
always last,
the second option.

When will my day come?

To be complete at heart
is to be somebody like you.

— Dusty Wilson

The Man in the Mirror
Identity

I don't know me.
I don't own me.

I want your love
out of my own self-pity.
It's not my responsibility.

I can't try to be
better than what I could see —

the man in the mirror.
That man is not me.

— Dusty Wilson

To Not Be Normal
Identity

I'd give up my life
to be normal —

my passion,
my drive,
my love,
and my lies —

all for your love.

I don't understand why you love them more,
and I don't know what to do.
My life is turning blue,
and I want to run to you —

but they hold me back with principality
and hate disguised as love.

You designed me for a purpose,
one that I cannot carry out —
yet you hate me for what I've become,
and I do not understand how to leave my image.

I can't escape my feelings.
I hate myself, and I do really love you.
I don't know why you don't try to change me.
I don't know why you made me.

—Dusty Wilson

Skin

Identity

Skin,
hair,
body —
I know you took more time on them.
Why couldn't you craft me
half as beautifully?

Stuck in my skin,
a body I don't know.
I'm stuck here waiting,
waiting to let go.

Skin,
hair,
body —
from my head to my toes.
I don't know why you made me —
why can't I just know?

— Dusty Wilson

Even Just Maybe
Identity

Even just maybe,
if you made me just a lady,
I could marry and be happy
and not be alone.

I hate myself—
and you so obviously hate me too.
I don't understand why.
I don't know what to do.

I can't escape my feelings;
you won't let me free.
Is this not animal cruelty,
with how everybody describes me?

Covered in hair—
and you couldn't care.
I don't understand how it's wrong to stare.

I just want what they have.
Maybe you're being cruel to be kind?
Maybe, just maybe,
I have just lost my mind.

—Dusty Wilson

Identity Dysmorphia

Identity

I don't understand.
I cannot escape my label
that this world confines me to.

Everybody hates me,
as they hated you too.

I don't understand why
you don't love me the same
way you love them —
and I don't know how to change.

I hate myself,
and I'm so, so sorry
I've become this way.

Why, oh why, did I have to be made of dismay?
I just want you to stay.
I love you so.

I'll change myself —
but even you won't change my heart, too.

—Dusty Wilson

I Have It All
Identity

A big house
and a beautiful yard —

but I'd give it all to be you
or anybody normal.

I want to have three kids
and a summer home.

Lead me on —
I don't even know.
I just wanna be normal.

— Dusty Wilson

Trapped Inside a Body
Identity

Trapped inside a body,
and you don't even care —
putting on my hair.

Why are you laughing at me,
trying not to stare?
Do you even know
what you've done?

I'm the laugh
of the town —
more than a clown,
less than myself.

When you love somebody,
there is nobody else.

—Dusty Wilson

Somebody Better
Identity

Don't say you know me
when you do not own me.
Don't say you know how I feel.

Must be somebody better —
somebody better for you.

I want to try,
don't want you to die,
but my heart can't take it
anymore.

I feel like a chore
to you.
I just want more
from you.

Sorry for hurting.
Why did you make me
if you would just hate me
for loving who I love?

— Dusty Wilson

Hometown
Identity / Nostalgia

Hometown—
moved up, away,
alone on that day
to a place that I couldn't call home.

I'm home-bound,
bound to a place that doesn't sit right.
I'm all alone—
no place to be known.

When I left my hometown—
a scent,
a smell,
a sound—
it all takes me back, hometown.

Baby, we're home-bound,
with no familiar sound.

—Dusty Wilson

Windrose
Identity / Longing / Place

The sun in the sky
and the birds in the air.
The wisp of a car —
that skyline stare.

Crooked sidewalks
and burning streets,
a daydream
that is always just too sweet.

I can't fall asleep,
I can't let go.
I can't call myself —
all I've known is *Windrose*.

I don't know why
you keep me down below.
I can't feel high —
there's only ever lows.

No matter what I do,
there's only *Windrose*.

A skylit smile,
a burning throw.
I know it makes sense,
but I can't let go.

I can only ever try
when you look in my eyes.
Can't you hold my hand,
if I'm just living to die?

Maybe I would be okay —
but this is going on forever.
While I look around,
you're holding me down
in each and every sever.

Every sickle in my heart —
God, why do you let them tear me apart?

You look at my life,
then you look away.
Your beloved —
stolen,
if only for another day.

— Dusty Wilson

Purple Hearts (Bruises)
Identity / Longing / Place

Saw you last week —
you were wearing those jeans.
I couldn't even bet,
look in your eyes,
tailored to my mind
with a little black silhouette.

Everything always hurts,
in the back of my mind.
I couldn't even begin to wonder why —
I wouldn't even curse you,
only cry.

When you look in my eyes
and tell me you love me,
that's when
I get my bruises.

—Dusty Wilson

SECTION II

OUTSIDE

Soccer Practice

OUTSIDE

I look around—
Those smiling faces,
Mothers sending their kids off
And giving a kiss to their husbands.

Practicing for this game
They've been playing their whole life—
If only they could get it right.
If only I could be like them,
Just for a night.

I wouldn't have to stay here,
Hiding in the light
Of the shadows in the halls.

The game whistle blows,
And the ball falls down.
I can't ever win—
I can't even try.
With all my might,
I can't say goodbye.

Their love, it kills me,
Knowing I can't just be happy.
I wish I could try—
I wish it wasn't a lie,
Or a daydream in my head.

Just remember—
We all bleed red.

— *Dusty Wilson*

Yellow School Bus

OUTSIDE

It's hard not to look and cry
When I just see a lie.
What I used to be
Has gone so far from me —

My age,
My face,
My skin,
My hair —
How could I ever compare?

— *Dusty Wilson*

On Friday Nights

OUTSIDE

When everybody's calling,
I can't wait for you —
Because you know I'm bawling.

Baby, baby please —
I can't help but want these.

Rather been a wife in the suburbs —
Three kids
And a Subaru.

For you, try to love me
When you're sitting there
Acting crazy.

How could I not compare our lives?
Why couldn't I have just been a wife?

That is what the sweet life is.
How can I not stare?
You just have it all there —
How could I compare?

— *Dusty Wilson*

Love Me, Oh Want Me

OUTSIDE

Love me like I want you back.
Love me— we're dumb,
And we've gone so long.

Love me
Before we're so washed up
And not beautiful.

Love me—
You hate me.
I want to be held.

— *Dusty Wilson*

Jealousy

OUTSIDE

I'm so jealous
Of your mirror —
It gets to stare at you a little longer.

I'm so jealous
Of your long, tan legs
That get to support such a beautiful body.

I'm so jealous
Of your eyes
That will always see what I never can —
So beautiful, so deep.

I love you,
And you don't even know me anymore.
How can I move on
When I'm so jealous
Of past times
When we were together —
So intimate,
So illegal?

I just wanted to love you —
What makes that wrong?
Why do you hate me so, so much?
I just wanted to run into your arms.

Wish we were
What we were before —

Back when I wasn't just a chore
To you.

Now I look in the mirror,
And all I can see is you.
I can't help but smile —
Because you make me so blue.

— Dusty Wilson

Numb

OUTSIDE

I don't even know
Why I like you,
Why I try to —
Be better off by yourself.

Don't you go calling me dumb;
I'm getting so numb without you, baby.

Let's listen to Kanye
And cry ourselves to sleep.

— *Dusty Wilson*

Midas

OUTSIDE

Everything you touch
Turns to gold —

Smiles on mirrors,
Talking for hours.

Baby,
Why you gotta go?

— *Dusty Wilson*

Drunken Hour

OUTSIDE

Only God knows
What she was doing in that hour —
So much more than a bottle.

Like a beautiful flower,
She couldn't see her worth.

— *Dusty Wilson*

Lovebug

OUTSIDE

Why would you make me —
Maybe even see me —
All my imperfections,
All my grace
And my wits' end?

You know what I like.
I love in a world forced full of love —
I just want you,
I just want to.

Please just let me love in this life.
I wanna be attracted,
I wanna feel attached to you —

Made in such a world
That hates me for what I see —
Love in my eyes
That don't even matter to you.

— *Dusty Wilson*

They're So Beautiful and I'm Just There

OUTSIDE

They're so beautiful,
And I'm just there.

I can't help but stare,
Or even compare.

How could you say
That you love me —
And make me into this?

I hate being
The second option
To everybody
And everyone.

I can't help it —
When I look in the mirror,
I can't see anything good,
Clearer — When the weather subsides
And I can't get out of my mind.

I hate my life,
And I just want to die.
That's where you'll find me —

In my heart,
In my life.

Why do you just try to cry
And pull me apart?
Why, my God, oh why?

— *Dusty Wilson*

Somebody, Anybody

OUTSIDE

Nobody wanted
This.

Nobody tried to love me
Before I tried to like this life.

I wanted to have a mansion—
A house in the sky.

When I tried,
I couldn't see the lies.

— Dusty Wilson

Ramirez

OUTSIDE

I loved you like a sister.
Tell me — were you with her?
Tell me it's not the mister.

At your lowest,
I was there.
Now you're higher than ever —
And you can't say hi.

— *Dusty Wilson*

SUBURBS

OUTSIDE

Trad wife
With a house in the suburbs —
Whiter than ice,
Blond with braces,
Making funny faces.

Baby, you think
You're going places.

But you hate this life you live
And I can't help —
Can't try to forgive.

— *Dusty Wilson*

The Price of Touch

OUTSIDE

Why do you have to dominate?
Push me down to a metal crate.

Am I worse to you
than all the other people combined?

Am I ready for
the rest of my life?
When will you have time
to realize you're killing me —
it's chivalry.

When will you try to see?
Just for a moment —
maybe just for me?

What did I ever do
to make you
this way?

Can't you try and just
look the other way at my dismay?

I can't try to go, can't try to stay.

Underneath a mistletoe —
but you only give sucker punches
instead of kisses.

In your defense,
it's on your wishlist.

— *Dusty Wilson*

SECTION III

PHILOSOPHY

PHILOSOPHY

The Scam of Free Will

PHILOSOPHY

He gave us free will,
yet everything we do is evil—
how can we please you?

I try so hard,
day and night,
to stop the evil things I do,
but it seems like every turn I make
is just another mistake.

The scam of free will—
how wicked we can be
when everyone
and everything
falls on me.

From ditching to turning,
stealing and lying,
loving and living—
when will we learn?

In the end I see
you with me.
You say, *If I am with you, who can be against you?*
yet you, yourself,
turn and ignore me.

I try to believe—
but how, oh how

can a relationship be
when you won't even talk to me?

Why do you lay these burdens
and look at me so?
I turn and cry,
and live in a lie.

All for a chance to love —
if it's not what we were made for,
then why were we made at all?

You knew we would fail,
treat me like a stepping stone
for your beloved to make it —
yet you say you love us *all the same.*

And that's why it hurts me so.
I try and I try,
just trying to sow
a seed
that I cannot even grow
in my own life,
just to help others
reach you on the other side.

So far away,
yet so deep within —
why, oh why, must my love be a sin?

Illegal to you,
yet you won't change me,
all for your stubbornness
and my lack of accountability.

I'm sorry I failed,
I'm sorry I tried —
I don't know how
to live in a lie.

Looking around and what do I see?
Everyone you loved —
and then there's just me.

If you knew I would fail,
yet you say that you love,
how is it just
that you made me
for lust?

You knew I would be
so wrong and in hell —
was it really love
if you knew I'd be damned?

Why, oh why,
do you create,
if not to destroy,
all for your justice —
and joy
that you plaster in love?

I'm just hurt
because I cry and I pray
that one day,
someday,
I might just understand.

The scam of free will.

— *Dusty Wilson*

What a Life It Is

PHILOSOPHY

What a life it is —
so wicked
and cruel.

Made to love,
but not made for you.

Although I love the truth,
it's a hard pill to swallow.
And I wish it would just go away,
and you could just stay
for another day —
one that I've never had,
and that I'll never get.

All because society,
and the fact you'd never like me.

I wish you could try to see —
but the veil sticks,
always against thee.

— *Dusty Wilson*

How Much Must I Toil and Tether

PHILOSOPHY

How much must I toil and tether —
just to find somebody
who knows me better?

Why, when I do it,
the world falls apart —
but *they* do nothing,
and their life is like art?

Why do you say
you love them more —
not with your voice,
but actions alone?

I don't understand
why you hate me so.
I guess if you want —
I can just go.

— *Dusty Wilson*

Nothing in Life Is Free

PHILOSOPHY

I've come to know
what's right
and what's true —
that people say
"nothing in life is free."

But I see it from a different perspective.

When a friend buys me a meal,
I pay in friendship.

When a birthday passes, I pay with my time.

But that which I cannot control
can't be measured by my own devices —
so who am I to be mad,
when my life isn't even my own?

When God paid in His own blood,
and I cherish the memories and moments.

So no, I don't reject
that nothing in life is free —

But I've been given free will
to give people love
and live freely- Which is ironic in a way,
because I can't see clearly
when people compare life
to their money.

— *Dusty Wilson*

The Downfall of Society

PHILOSOPHY

The downfall of society
is not what it seems —

with AI and chatbots,
and fake bodies,
beautiful crooked teeth
that we traded
for plastic veneers.

But worst of all
is the falsity of human descent —

the lie that every person
cannot grow and change.

People put themselves in boxes
and blame their actions
on their parents.

But as I've grown,
I've come to know
that *we can change.*

And as a society,
we don't have to follow
these ways —

the very ones
that destroyed
a generation of people.

Therapists don't treat
the people who need it—
they treat their victims.

And that's what hurts the most.

— *Dusty Wilson*

The Lack of Encouragement

PHILOSOPHY

Nothing is as it seems —
that goes to show
when people value

fake teeth,
and "perfect" bodies
wrapped in fine linen,
yet discarded in trash.

How can we know?
Taking turns with a clash?

But the worst of it all
is not what it seems —
not at all.
Not even a perfect body.

That box we see —
that *freedom* —
we give away for comfortability.

To take what we're given
without testing our limits,
the things our parents instilled
that were false
in themselves.

The thought that we
can't think freely —

therapists do not treat
those who need it,
but rather
their victims.

That is what has destroyed
an entire generation,
while the whole world laughs,
knowing they'll make
a quick buck.

The profit of an ego death,
sold for security —
vain as can be,
and truthfully,
not worth the money.

— *Dusty Wilson*

That's Just the Way Life Is

PHILOSOPHY

That's just the way life is —
people take
until there is nothing left
to hold.

They say, *"be patient,"*
but patience never held me
when I cried myself to sleep.

They say, *"be grateful,"*
yet nothing grows
in soil that never belonged to me.

I watch the world feast
while I starve
on hope and apologies.

They say,
"it gets better,"
but better never came —
only older.

Maybe that's the trick:
life never promised joy,
just breath —
and breath is not a promise
of living.

So I stopped waiting
for the good part.

Maybe life isn't meant
to be loved —
only survived.

— *Dusty Wilson*

Section IV

LOVE

Boyfriend, Boyfriend

LOVE

Boyfriend, boyfriend — be me.
I don't wanna see
what you're doing to me.

Boyfriend — be me.
Baby, I can't see.
Come and do it to me again.

I can't date myself
or love you even harder,
especially for free.

— *Dusty Wilson*

Lover Boy

LOVE

Torture by my own love
is forbidden.
I've been forgotten.

Forever
I'll remember
the way you looked at me.

It's illegal, don't you know?
What they'll say,
what he'll do
if he finds me with you.

— *Dusty Wilson*

To Have a Best Friend

LOVE

Go on a drive
to clear my mind.
Hope your farewells
won't be too kind.

In glitter and postcards
and Lerner & Rowe.
Your sweet little smile —
I can't let go.

Get me a coffee,
no creamer in mind.
We sit there for hours —
leave me high and dry.

I cannot try
to read your kind —
your vulnerability and stupidity,
I cannot try.

Two different pawns —
part of the same set.
When will you realize?
And try not to regret?

Take her over me,
mistakenly.
She can't even know — or try to let go.

Her burden and grasp —
and you even relapsed.

— *Dusty Wilson*

Fawn

LOVE

Roses in the sky,
your pink leather clouds.
When can we all
just try to be aloud?

Wayward son —
can't find his way home,
can't wait to be alone.

Can you try to let go?
Because it's killing me —
can't you see
what you've done to me?

These black shoes
can seem to get to you —
I couldn't run,
even if I tried to.

In sunlit parks
and cheap perfume —
your favorite hair,
my *try-to-let-you*,
can't seem to wait this out,
just wanna get you.

— *Dusty Wilson*

Zero

LOVE

Everywhere, all at once —
in her mind.
She swore,
she tried —
but then forget.
Can't even realize.

The doctors say it's doomsday.
Why can't you try to relay?
I can't let go —
you need to know —
here comes another replay.

You zero out
and hold it in.
I cannot try,
I cannot try,
try to pretend.

We cannot lie —
but for your sake,
you can't even remember your
wake —

Wake up
in the morning,
the same day it's been for years.
The sun shining over your ears,
who knew it'd be
our worst fears?

You can't drop dead —
where is another?
Who else could I call
my mother?
Even if you were another —

Zero.

— *Dusty Wilson*

High and Low

LOVE

I see God in other people.
I've searched the highest mountains
and the deepest seas —

only Your love
was ever found
with me.

Frail old man
walking down the street—
smiles at you,
and right back at me.

I see Him in other people,
high and low —
You always show
for me.

Lord, I love You,
above all else.
You will always prevail.

In dark waters
of the deep blue sea,
Your love will always
shine on me.

Highest mountains —
I'll show You why
I love my Lord,
my God,
Almighty.

I see God in everything.
High and low —
You always show.

— *Dusty Wilson*

The Devil Is a Liar

LOVE

The devil told you a lie —
and yet you still wonder why
you have that plank
in your eye.

You think you weren't made to serve
the One
who created you.

— *Dusty Wilson*

Truth

LOVE

They tell them what they want to hear
and bury Your word
in the back of their mind.

They know You are kind,
but they are too selfish
to realize.

— *Dusty Wilson*

This Love

LOVE

They say that Your love is free for most,
but for me it costs me my hope for a better future.

I'm giving up my love and family —
and the ability to wake up with my husband
in the middle of the night on Christmas Eve
and place presents under the tree for our kids.

My life has been taken from me for You,
yet I still feel casted away.

What did I do to deserve this from You?
Why are they so different from me?

The craziest part about it all
is that even after all of this,
You still turn away,
no matter how much I grieve the loss of my future.

No matter how brokenhearted I am,
I still feel unrepairable
and thrown into the fire.

Why must I pay such a high price
compared to every other Christian?

Why do You love them more
than You have loved me?

Truly, I tell You —
if how You love is considered right
in the eyes of the Lord,
You are blessed beyond belief.

In the same light,
if it is not,
your own conscience will eat away at you
and make you as unsettled
as the place where there is suffering
and gnashing of weeping teeth.

— *Dusty Wilson*

Getting Older

LOVE

One day
these wrinkles
will be seen as more than imperfection.

One day —
a sign of wisdom.

Someday
this gray hair
won't weigh down my heart
and tear me apart.

Someday, someday —
I'm falling apart.

I feel old
and dry,
no way in my mind.

I can't see the sky —
these eyes are turning blind.

On the bright side,
I'm closer to release,
so I can see you again
on the flip side.

— *Dusty Wilson*

Have You No Pity?

LOVE / HYPOCRISY

You have the life I've always wanted,
as you pick mine apart
and leave me dry.

You preach forgiveness
but never to me.

You speak of love,
but only when the audience is watching.

You get to enjoy the simple things in life
while I watch and die.

— *Dusty Wilson*

PLEASE DON'T TELL ME THAT THE PRICE IS TOO MUCH TO PAY

LOVE

Please don't tell me that the price
is too much to pay
for somebody like you.

On that day,
I'll sit there and wait
while everybody prospers.

Why am I last?
Why couldn't we last?

I thought love was better,
but my life fell apart—
and I couldn't ever
put myself back together.

— *Dusty Wilson*

Every Offering I Gave You

LOVE

Ignored.
Why, oh why,
am I just a chore to you?

I just want your love —
but my heart can't compare
when I was just there,
and stuck up in your hair.

How could I compare
when they have got it all figured out?

Why haven't you thrown me out?
Why do you hate me,
but still hold on?

Why do you love me,
but lead me to somebody else?

Why can't I love myself?
What did I do to deserve this?

Why can't you just pick up the phone
when I'm all alone?

And you don't try to save me
when I can't even save myself —
let alone somebody else.

Trust me, it shows.
I know you don't really love me.

— Dusty Wilson

A Bed of Daisies

LOVE

Lay with me
and tell me a lie.
Let me hope
I could love for a night.

If I couldn't let it happen —
if not for a second —
I couldn't know what love is,
not in your reflection.

A salt to my wound,
a heart of gold.
More pure than life,
and a mirror of my ego death.

As I sit here
and I lay to rest
in this bed of daisies,
the stars in the sky
are nothing in comparison to your eyes.

Yet I cannot see —
you will never be with me.
If only in my mind,
could you let me live this lie?
If only for a night
in my bed of daisies —
with only enough room
for somebody like me.

— Dusty Wilson

Mother, May I?
FAMILY

Inside these walls,
this tomb of a house —
not a creak is heard,
or the scurry of a mouse.

In a cave of my own misery,
if not right where I belong —
someone as wretched as me,
I try not to long.

The love from my mother
that has grown ever so bitter
eats away at my heart —
a wither and tither.

A wayward son
cannot find his way
in a place like this,
a house — not a home.

So I weep and I cry,
I try to sleep through the night —
but make sure not to wake her,
if even out of spite.

Trust me, I know —
her hit is worse than a bite.

Oh mother, please —
may I?

— Dusty Wilson

My Life
FAMILY

I hate my job —
but at least I have one.
I hate being single —
but at least I live in America.

I feel so privileged
that I have no room to cry
when there's some kid in Sierra Leone
who can barely find enough food for the day,
or a little girl just born in North Korea
who was born with all odds against her.

How can I be sad
when I live like this?
How can I be happy
without being pretentious?

How can my problems
be anything at all
when, in comparison,
I can't ever be enough —
but they can't get enough to live?

So how can it be?
I'm worried about who's looking at me
when they're worried about
living another day
in this hell called life
that I just wanted to numb down with love —
a love that was never meant for me.

But how could I compare?
When their problems may be theirs,
but mine never will compare.

I can't cry.
I can't even try to be happy
without feeling bad about myself.

So I'm sorry —
I lived in this cruel world
that has torn me apart,
even though the Silicon Valley
has made my soul feel like silk sheets and linen —
soft yet brittle,
and nothing in comparison.

— Dusty Wilson

I Want to Be a Dad
FAMILY

I want to be a dad —
but I want to stay a kid.
I look around at all,
and all is what it is.

Everyone else
seems so ready
to grow into their lives.
I still feel like a child
trapped inside
a body that's aging too fast.

I want to teach someone
how to ride a bike,
tie their shoes,
pray before bed.
But I still forget
to take care of myself.

I want to give the love
I never received.
I want to break the cycle —
even when I feel
like I'm still stuck inside it.

I want to be a dad —
but I don't know how to stop
being the kid
who never got held.

— Dusty Wilson

Beautiful

FAMILY

I see beauty in everything.
Hatred stems from her heart.

Pull me—
pull me apart,
tear at my heart.

From heaven to an art.

— *Dusty Wilson*

Section V

SOCIETY

Rich and Wrapped in Plastic
SOCIETY

You're the richest —
top .1%.
You say you mean
every word you meant,
but not really.
Even it is sold
to the ones above —
can't get old,
can't sell my soul,
can't think to myself,
or even see gold.

The poor of the rich,
all for the fame —
think that everybody
knows your name.

— *Dusty Wilson*

Golden Statues
SOCIETY

You say you're building a life —
but all I see are landfills wrapped in linen.
Golden statues for the rich,
and I'm the silent witness.

You come home late,
smelling like dreams that weren't ours.

"I'm just now getting off work," you say —
but your shirt tells the truth
before your mouth ever does.

We used to talk about Grammys,
and a house in the Hamptons.
"Life was good,"
you'd say.
But only for you.

I thought we were building something —
but we were just *building you.*

You chase the cameras,
I chase your ghost.
You get applause,
I get the cold side of the bed.

You trade devotion
for trophies on the mantle.
You trade me
for someone newer.

"How dare you,"
I whisper —

but not to you.
To the world that tells you
it's normal.

People are dying,
ecosystems collapsing,
but your biggest worry
is whether your suit looks expensive enough
for the photos.

You talk of saving the world
while stepping on mine.

Refilling landfill dreams
with dollar signs,
promising prophecy
with practiced speeches.

You don't want love —
you want worship.

You don't want me —
you want a statue.

Divorce sounds like mercy.
Freedom sounds like truth.

Put me in a golden statue,
so you can say you never broke me.
But we both know
you melted me down
to build your kingdom.

— Dusty Wilson

SECTION VI

WARFARE

Green Mile
WARFARE

I dream about you
in a green mile.
Sit down for a while —
why won't you?
Or rather, would you?

I can't try to.
They keep coming,
they keep running —
that green mile,
oh, that skyline smile.

Looking around —
all the people I've helped —
now we're going through hell.
What are we fighting for?
I don't wanna be here anymore.

— *Dusty Wilson*

As the World Still Spins
WARFARE

as the world still spins
as the flowers bloom
and hummingbirds loom
a beautiful room

oh, it's so hard to grieve.

what we had
and what was never to come
left for dead, or maybe just a hum —
a whisper in my ear
as my world goes deaf.

my heart grows cold,
the songs speak of death.

how could I ever?
as my feet grow weary
I can't imagine seeking help —
I can't imagine leering.

looking for a love
is worse than a light in a darkness
after you've been blinded
through the shields of stone.

a stillness of heart,
a world alone.

a world still spins
as a heart comes to atone.

— Dusty Wilson

Godforsaken
WARFARE

as the tears fall down
onto the page,
I regret everything I said
on that day.

maybe I was too harsh,
but know it was the truth.
my heart grows cold,
and my worrisome too.

hopefully not forever —
if you could find time to forgive.
maybe me, I could help —
maybe find time to live.

when you feel so numb
and you can't come down,
just lay down,
let your heart come out.

to scream from the rooftops
is ever so bold.
a heart can ache,
but love can't grow old —
or so, I've been told.

— Dusty Wilson

Your Sacrifice
WARFARE

I tried and I tried,
I wept and I cried—
saying, *"give me a sign."*

and You opened Your arms
and died.

for somebody like me?
how could I ever be worthy?

Amen.

— Dusty Wilson

www.ingramcontent.com/pod-product-compliance
Lightning Source LLC
Chambersburg PA
CBHW031245120626
46545CB00007B/2652